D1385085

★ ★

GEORGIA

by Andrea Murphy

GARETH**STEVENS**

GS

PUBLISHING

A Member of the WRC Media Family of Companies

Please visit our web site at: www.garethstevens.com
For a free color catalog describing Gareth Stevens Publishing's
list of high-quality books and multimedia programs, call
1-800-542-2595 (USA) or 1-800-387-3178 (Canada).
Gareth Stevens Publishing's fax: (414) 332-3567.

Library of Congress Cataloging-in-Publication Data

Murphy, Andrea, 1947-
    Georgia / Andrea Murphy.
        p. cm. — (Portraits of the states)
    Includes bibliographical references and index.
    ISBN 0-8368-4623-0 (lib. bdg.)
    ISBN 0-8368-4642-7 (softcover)
    1. Georgia—Juvenile literature. I. Title. II. Series.
    F286.3.M86   2005
    975.8—dc22   2005042663

This edition first published in 2006 by
Gareth Stevens Publishing
A Member of the WRC Media Family of Companies
330 West Olive Street, Suite 100
Milwaukee, WI 53212 USA

This edition copyright © 2006 by Gareth Stevens, Inc.

Editorial direction: Mark J. Sachner
Project manager: Jonatha A. Brown
Editor: Betsy Rasmussen
Art direction and design: Tammy West
Picture research: Diane Laska-Swanke
Indexer: Walter Kronenberg
Production: Jessica Morris and Robert Kraus

Picture credits: Cover, pp. 4, 22 © Graeme Teague; p. 5 © Corel; p. 6 © North
Wind Picture Archives; pp. 8, 24, 25 © Library of Congress; p. 10 © MPI/Getty
Images; p. 12 © Donald Uhrbrock/Time & Life Pictures/Getty Images; p. 15
© PhotoDisc; p. 16 Courtesy of Morehouse College; p. 21 © James P. Rowan;
p. 26 Macon-Bibb County Convention & Visitors Bureau; p. 27 © Gibson Stock
Photography; p. 28 Columbus Convention & Visitors Bureau; p. 29 © National
Baseball Hall of Fame Library/MLB Photos via Getty Images

Printed in the United States of America

1 2 3 4 5 6 7 8 9 09 08 07 06 05

CONTENTS

Words that are defined in the Glossary appear
in **bold** the first time they are used in the text.

On the Cover: Many visitors to Georgia come to tour old
homes like this one.

Introduction

Called "The Peach State," Georgia is known for its sweet, juicy peaches. It is also known for many natural places. Georgia is home to the largest **swamp** in North America. It also has a famous **gorge** that is very long and deep.

Many famous people came from Georgia, too. Jackie Robinson, who was the first African American to play major league baseball, came from Georgia. So did Martin Luther King Jr. He helped African Americans get equal rights. Jimmy Carter is from Georgia, too. He became a U.S. president. He has worked for many years to bring peace to the world.

So, welcome to Georgia! It is a great state to explore.

Georgia's peach trees produce fruit from mid-May to August. That is only sixteen weeks each year!

The state flag of Georgia.

GEORGIA FACTS

- Became the 4th State: January 2, 1788
- Population (2004): 8,829,383
- Capital: Atlanta
- Biggest Cities: Atlanta, Augusta-Richmond, Columbus, Savannah
- Size: 58,910 square miles (152,577 square kilometers)
- Nickname: The Peach State
- State Tree: Live oak
- State Flower: Cherokee rose
- State Bird: Brown thrasher
- State Crop: Peanut

CHAPTER 2

History

Native Americans came to what is now Georgia thousands of years ago. They hunted animals and gathered plants to eat. When the first Europeans arrived, about one dozen Native groups lived there. The largest groups were the Creek and the Cherokee.

The Spanish sailed along the Georgia coast in 1521. About twenty years later, Hernando de Soto explored the area. The Spanish built settlements along the coast. They also built **missions** so they could teach the Natives about their God. The Spanish called Georgia *Guale* (wah lee), after a Native chief.

Native Americans welcome James Oglethorpe and the first English settlers to Georgia in 1733.

The British wanted the land, too. They began attacking the Spanish. By 1686, Spain had lost most of Georgia.

The Georgia Colony

In 1732, the British set up the **colony** of Georgia. They named it for King George II. The next year, they began to

Oglethorpe and the Georgia Colony

James Oglethorpe made laws for Georgia that no other colony had. He outlawed slavery. He did not let people buy and sell large pieces of land. Some colonists did not like these laws. They forced Oglethorpe to change them. They created plantations and used African slaves to work in the fields.

FUN FACTS

History Mystery

Natives known as Mound Builders once lived in Georgia. They built large mounds of earth in their settlements. They may have used these mounds as bases for buildings. No one knows for sure what happened to the Mound Builders. They disappeared before white people came to Georgia. It is a mystery to this day.

settle the colony. James Oglethorpe took about one hundred settlers to the coast. They founded the town of Savannah. It was the first long-lasting white settlement in Georgia. The colony began to produce rice, pork, sugar, and more. Many people there grew rich.

Britain held thirteen colonies along the Atlantic Coast. The colonists grew tired of British rule. They started a war for freedom from Britain in 1775. It was the Revolutionary War. Georgia joined the fight. The colonists won the war and formed the United States. In 1788, Georgia became the fourth U.S. state.

The Trail of Tears

The United States fought Britain again in the War of 1812. During this war, Creek Natives sided with the British. The U.S. Army beat the Creek in a few big battles in Georgia. Afterward, the Creek gave up most of their

Workers pick cotton in a Georgia cotton field in 1917. Many workers could pick more than two hundred pounds of cotton a day.

land in the state. By 1827, they had lost all their lands. They were forced to move to Oklahoma.

The Cherokee did better for a while. They kept most of their land in the north of Georgia. They learned to dress and live like white people. Some rich Cherokee even owned slaves. In 1828, gold was discovered on Cherokee lands. The state soon took over the land and gave it to white settlers. In 1838, the U.S. Army made more than eighteen thousand Cherokee leave the state. They had to march to Oklahoma. The journey was very long. Thousands of Natives died along the way. This terrible trip is known as the "Trail of Tears."

The Civil War

By 1800, cotton was grown throughout the state. Most of it was planted and picked by slaves. By this time, almost half the people in the state were slaves.

FACTS

King Cotton

In 1793, Eli Whitney invented the cotton gin in Georgia. His gin took seeds out of cotton. It did the work that once had been done by hand. More and more people planted cotton. Many of these farmers grew rich. Cotton became known as "king" in the South.

IN GEORGIA'S HISTORY

Sherman in Georgia

General William T. Sherman fought for the North in the Civil War. His army took Atlanta in 1864. To hurt the South, he burned as much of Atlanta as he could. Next, he headed toward the coast. Along the way, his army destroyed houses, factories, and railroads. They burned crops and barns. This was a terrible time for Georgia.

Many people in the North wanted to stop slavery. People in Georgia and the rest of the South did not. In 1861, Southern states broke away and formed their own country. They became the Confederate States of America. Northern states did not want southern states to leave the **Union**. The two sides began the Civil War in 1861.

In 1865, the South lost the war. Georgia was in

ruins. It took many years for the state to recover.

Before the Civil War, Atlanta was a big transportation center. In 1864, General Sherman's army destroyed Atlanta's railroad.

Hard Times

Georgia was once again part of the Union. Slavery was

IN GEORGIA'S HISTORY

A Cotton Disaster

In 1913, an insect called the boll weevil attacked the state. Its main food was cotton. In the early 1920s, it destroyed most of the cotton crop. Many farmers lost everything. Thousands of people left their farms and moved north to find work. This was called the Great Migration.

against the law. Even so, many white people did not treat black people as equals. They passed laws to keep black people away from them. These laws said that blacks and whites must use different restaurants, parks, bathrooms, and schools. Georgia was **segregated**.

The bad times went on and on. Many people lost their jobs and their money during the **Great Depression**. The whole country was in trouble, and Georgia was one of the poorest states.

The United States entered World War II in 1941. The military needed airplanes, ships, and guns to fight the war. It also needed places to train soldiers. Georgia was ready to help. **Factories** in the state made equipment for the war. Military bases were built there, too. Soon, thousands of soldiers were being trained in Georgia. These changes brought jobs to the state.

African American Hopes and Dreams

After the war, life was good for many Georgians. Yet black people were still not treated fairly. African Americans began to speak out against segregation. Atlanta became a center of the **Civil Rights** Movement, which sought to end segregation. In 1954, the U.S. Supreme Court said that public schools must be open to children of all races. Even so, schools in Georgia were slow to change. Finally, black and white children began going to the same schools in 1961.

In 1972, Georgia took a big step forward. It elected

IN GEORGIA'S HISTORY

Olympic Games

In 1996, the Summer Olympic Games were held in Atlanta. Such a big event took years of planning. The games were a huge success. They drew **tourists** to the state from all over the world. More than ten thousand athletes competed in the 271 events.

Famous People of Georgia

Dr. Martin Luther King Jr.

Born: January 15, 1929, Atlanta, Georgia

Died: April 4, 1968, Memphis, Tennessee

Martin Luther King Jr. grew up in Atlanta. He was African American. In the 1950s and 1960s, he spoke out against segregation. Dr. King urged black people to work peacefully for change. In just a few years, he earned the respect and love of people of all races. He became famous as a civil rights leader. In 1964, he won the Nobel Peace Prize for his civil rights work. He was killed on April 4, 1968. We now honor Dr. King every year on the third Monday of January.

a black man, Andrew Young, to the U.S. Congress. In 2002, Shirley Franklin made history. She became the first woman to be mayor of Atlanta. She was also the first black woman ever to be mayor of a big city in the southeast.

Today, Georgia is known as a great place to live, work, and play.

Dr. Martin Luther King Jr. gave many powerful speeches. His words helped make life better for black people.

★ ★ ★ Time Line ★ ★ ★

1540	Explorer Hernando de Soto comes to Georgia.
1733	James Edward Oglethorpe starts Georgia colony at Savannah.
1788	Georgia becomes the fourth state.
1793	Eli Whitney invents the cotton gin.
1821	Sequoyah invents a Cherokee alphabet.
1838–1839	Cherokee are driven from their land.
1861	Georgia joins the Confederate States of America.
1861–1865	The Civil War is fought.
1913	The boll weevil arrives in Georgia and begins to destroy the cotton crop.
1929–1940	The Great Depression hits Georgia's economy hard.
1941	U.S. involvement in World War II begins.
1976	Jimmy Carter of Georgia is elected U.S. president.
2002	Jimmy Carter wins the Nobel Peace Prize.
2005	Jackie Robinson wins the Congressional Gold Medal.

People

Georgia is growing faster than most states. Almost nine million people live there. Almost half of them live in or near Atlanta.

People come to Georgia for many reasons. Some come to work in Georgia's cities. Others leave their homes in states with colder climates to **retire** in Georgia. People come to Georgia from other countries, too. Recently, many people have moved to the state from Mexico, India, and Vietnam.

Hispanics: In the 2000 U.S. Census, 5.3 percent of the people in Georgia called themselves Latino or Hispanic. Most of them or their relatives came from places where Spanish is spoken. They may come from different racial backgrounds.

The People of Georgia

Total Population 8,829,383

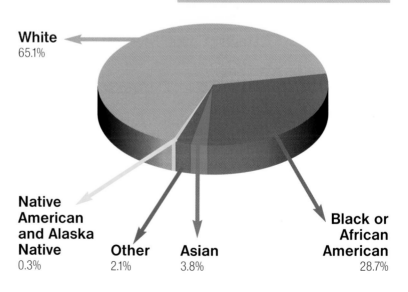

White
65.1%

Native American and Alaska Native
0.3%

Other
2.1%

Asian
3.8%

Black or African American
28.7%

Percentages are based on 2000 Census.

Car lights streak below the skyline of Atlanta, Georgia's capital and largest city.

Georgia's African Americans, Natives, and Hispanics

In the mid-1800s, about half of the people in Georgia were African American. After the slaves were freed, most could not find decent jobs. Many went north in hopes of finding a better way of life. Since then, Georgia has changed. Many blacks now come to Georgia for better lives. In the state

FUN FACTS

Talking Leaves

Sequoyah was a Cherokee. He lived in Georgia as a young man. His people did not have a written language. He could read and write. He understood that writing was a powerful tool. In 1821, he made a Cherokee alphabet. He called it "Talking Leaves." Many Cherokee learned this alphabet. Soon, they were printing their own newspaper. Many Cherokee still use this alphabet today.

Students and teachers parade as part of their graduation from Morehouse College.

today, about three people in ten are black. Most of them live in cities. Now, more than half of the people in Atlanta and Savannah are African Americans.

Very few Natives still live in Georgia. The number of Hispanics there is small but growing.

Education and Religion

Until 1872, the state was too poor to pay for public schools. That year, the state began paying for public grade schools. It began paying for public high schools in 1912. Black and white children attended separate schools until the 1960s.

Georgia has many colleges and universities. It has a

large state university system. This system includes thirty-four schools.

The Atlanta University Center is a famous group of schools. Its schools were first set up to serve African Americans. These schools led the way in higher education for black people.

Most people in Georgia are Christian. More than half of these people are Baptists. The second largest group is Methodist. Other Christians in Georgia include Catholics. When Georgia first became a colony, the colonists did not allow Catholics to move there. The first permanent Catholic church was founded there in the late 1700s.

A small group of Jews have been present in the state from the beginning.

Famous People of Georgia

Juliette Gordon Low

Born: October 31, 1860, Savannah, Georgia

Died: January 17, 1927, Savannah, Georgia

Juliette Gordon Low visited England. She met the founder of the Boy Scouts and Girl Guides. In 1912, Low started the first U.S. Girl Guide Troop in Savannah. It became the Girl Scouts in 1913. Girl Scouts learned about nature. They learned that they could grow up to do almost any job they wanted. The Girl Scouts started with eighteen girls. Today, there are more than three million Girl Scouts.

CHAPTER
★ ★ ★ ★ ★ ★ ★

The Land

Georgia is the largest state east of the Mississippi River. It is made up of different regions with different landscapes.

The northern part of Georgia has mountains and valleys, but they cover only a small portion of the state. The Appalachian Mountains start there, and they run all the way to Maine. The state's highest mountain is Brasstown Bald. It is in a part of the Appalachians known as the Blue Ridge Mountains. It is 4,784 feet (1,458 meters) high.

The **Piedmont** region lies a bit further south. It covers about one-third of the state. Gentle hills roll across most of the Piedmont. Farms are found where the land is flatter. Pine forests cover the higher hills.

South of the Piedmont are the plains. They cover more than half of the state. The land there is mostly flat. It is used for farming. Some hills stand in the northern part of this area. **Salt marshes** are found along the Atlantic coast. Many freshwater swamps lie farther inland, including the Okefenokee swamp.

GEORGIA

TENNESSEE

Trail of Tears

NORTH CAROLINA

Russell Cave NM

Chickamauga and
Chattanooga NMP

Brasstown Bald Mt.
L. Burton

Blue Ridge Mountains

Appalachian Mountains

Etowah
Indian
Mounds

Etowah R.

Amicalola Falls
Hartwell L.
L. •Gainsville

Sidney
Lanier

Allatoona L.

SOUTH
CAROLINA

Kennesaw
Mountain NBP

Chattahoochee R.

•Athens
Chattahoochee River NRA

J. Strom
Thurmond L.

★ •Atlanta Stone
Mountain
Park

Jackson L.

Augusta•

L. Sinclair

N

W   E

S

•Milledgeville

Savannah R.

West Point L.

Flint R.

•Macon
Ocmulgee NM

Oconee R.

ALABAMA

L. Harding
•Columbus

Ocmulgee R.

Andersonville NHS
•Vienna

Savannah•
Fort Pulaski NM
Midway•

Plains•
Providence
Canyon SP

L. Blackshear

Altamaha R.

L. Worth

Flint R.

Satilla R.

L. Seminole

Hahira•

•Cairo

Alapaha R.

Suwannee R.

St. Marys R.

Okefenokee
Swamp

Cumberland
Island NS

ATLANTIC
OCEAN

SCALE/KEY

0	100 Miles
0	100 Kilometers

FLORIDA

✪ State Capital

▲ Highest Point

▨ Mountains

Climate

The climate in the plains is usually warm and humid. In the mountains, the weather is cooler. Sometimes

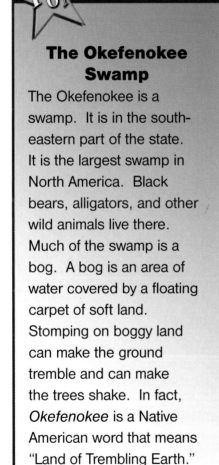

Major Rivers

Chattahoochee River
436 miles (702 km) long

Savannah River
314 miles (505 km) long

Suwannee River
250 miles (402 km) long

hurricanes slam into the state, causing damage.

Waterways

Georgia has many rivers. The rivers in the north and eastern part of the state flow to the Atlantic Ocean. The rivers in the south and west flow to the Gulf of Mexico.

The northern part of the state has many waterfalls. The highest is Amicalola Falls. *Amicalola* is a Cherokee word that means "tumbling waters."

Plants and Animals

About two-thirds of the state

FUN FACTS

The Okefenokee Swamp

The Okefenokee is a swamp. It is in the south-eastern part of the state. It is the largest swamp in North America. Black bears, alligators, and other wild animals live there. Much of the swamp is a bog. A bog is an area of water covered by a floating carpet of soft land. Stomping on boggy land can make the ground tremble and can make the trees shake. In fact, *Okefenokee* is a Native American word that means "Land of Trembling Earth."

is covered with forests. Pine trees are common in the western forests.

Many different kinds of plants grow in the state. Salt marsh grasses grow along the Atlantic coast. They provide food and shelter for sea animals. Tupelo, red gum, and cypress trees grow in the swamps. The swamps are also home to waterbirds.

Raccoons, rabbits, and other small mammals are found across the state. The lakes and rivers are filled with freshwater fish. A few black bears are found in the mountains and forests.

FACTS

Where the Wild Things Are

Cumberland Island lies off the coast of Georgia. It is the largest undeveloped island on the East Coast. People lucky enough to visit will often find sea turtles there. They can see wild turkeys, armadillos, and wild horses, too. The island is very natural. There are no stores, and there are very few cars and people. It is a nature lover's delight.

Floating islands covered with trees and shrubs dot the Okefenokee Swamp.

Economy

Atlanta is home to many big businesses. United Parcel Service (UPS), Delta Air Lines, and CNN have their main offices in Atlanta. Coca-Cola, which was invented in Atlanta, has its main offices there, too.

The city is also a big transportation center. Most of the major highways and railroads in the Southeast run through Atlanta. Its airport is one of the busiest in the world.

Georgia's factories make baked goods, soft drinks, and peanut butter. Some factories make **textiles**. Georgia produces

A peanut farmer works in the fields. Peanuts grow underground and are sometimes called ground nuts.

about one-half of the carpets made in the United States. Other factories make cars and equipment for airplanes and spacecraft.

Tourism also brings money to the state. It brings jobs, too. Hotels, restaurants, and tourist spots all need workers.

Farms, Forests, and More

Georgia is home to about fifty thousand farms. From farming, chickens and peanuts bring in the most money. Georgia is one of the top producers in the country of broiler chickens. Georgia grows more peanuts than any other U.S. state. Cotton, peaches, and pecans are big crops, too.

Georgia's forests provide wood for lumber and paper. Mines produce stone and clay. Georgia produces more clay than any other state.

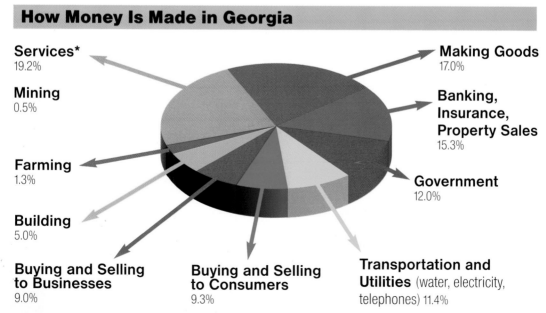

How Money Is Made in Georgia

Services* 19.2%

Mining 0.5%

Farming 1.3%

Building 5.0%

Buying and Selling to Businesses 9.0%

Buying and Selling to Consumers 9.3%

Transportation and Utilities (water, electricity, telephones) 11.4%

Government 12.0%

Banking, Insurance, Property Sales 15.3%

Making Goods 17.0%

* Services include jobs in hotels, restaurants, auto repair, medicine, teaching, and entertainment.

Government

$\mathbf{A}$tlanta is the capital of Georgia. The state's leaders work there. The state government has three parts, or branches. They are the executive, legislative, and judicial branches.

Executive Branch

The governor is head of this branch. The lieutenant governor helps run the branch. They make sure state laws are carried out. Many other officials also work in this branch.

Georgia's state capitol was completed in 1889. Ten U.S. states have gold domes on their capitol buildings, but Georgia's is the largest.

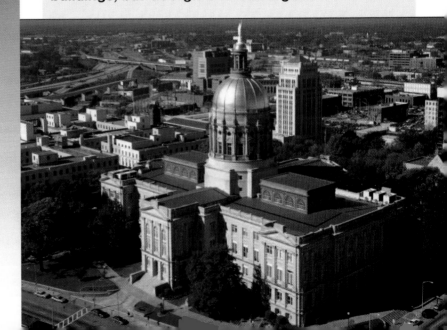

The Old State Capitol Building in Milledgeville, Georgia's capital city before the Civil War.

Legislative Branch

The legislative branch makes state laws. The legislature has two parts. One is the Senate. The other is the House of Representatives. The two work together as the General Assembly.

Judicial Branch

Judges and courts make up the judicial branch. Judges and courts may decide whether people who have been **accused of** committing crimes are guilty.

Local Government

Georgia is divided into 159 counties. Most counties are run by a group of people called a board of commissioners. Most towns and cities are run by boards as well.

GEORGIA'S STATE GOVERNMENT

Executive		Legislative		Judicial	
Office	**Length of Term**	**Body**	**Length of Term**	**Court**	**Length of Term**
Governor	4 years	Senate (56 members)	2 years	Supreme (7 judges)	6 years
Lieutenant Governor	4 years	House of Representatives (180 members)	2 years	Appeals (12 judges)	6 years

Things to See and Do

Georgia has many historic areas. The Chieftains Trail runs through the northwest part of the state. It shows the history of Native Americans in Georgia. The Antebellum Trail runs through Macon, Athens, and other towns. On this trail, people see what life was like in the state before the Civil War.

The Martin Luther King Jr. National Historic Site is in Atlanta. It tells about King's fight for civil rights. Seabrook Historical Village

FUN FACTS

The Sea Islands

The Sea Islands off the coast are rich with history. A group of freed slaves lived on these lovely islands for many years. These people were called the Gullah. They had their own language and their own way of life.

A young visitor visits the Earthlodge at the Ocmulgee National Monument in Macon.

Jimmy Carter

Born: October 1, 1924, Plains, Georgia

James Earl Carter grew up on his family's farm. He did chores and was a good student. Later, he became a peanut farmer. He served as a state senator and then became governor of Georgia. In 1976, he was elected as the thirty-ninth U.S. president. He served for one term. Since then, he has helped build homes for poor people and has worked for world peace. In 2002, he won the Nobel Peace Prize. He won this prize for helping people all over the world.

is in Midway. Visitors there can see what life was like for African Americans in Georgia after the Civil War.

Museums

The High Museum of Art is in Atlanta. This museum has African and American art. Children who visit there can use maps with interesting clues to go on treasure hunts.

The High Museum of Art in Atlanta is one of the top art museums in the Southeastern United States.

Famous People of Georgia

Jackie Robinson

Born: January 31, 1919, Cairo, Georgia

Died: October 24, 1972, Stamford, Connecticut

Jackie Robinson was an African American. He loved sports and wanted to play professional baseball. At the time, black people were not allowed to play in the major leagues. Jackie made history in 1947. That year, he became the first black player in the majors. He was a great hitter. He helped the Brooklyn Dodgers win the World Series in 1955. Later in life, he worked for civil rights. In March 2005, the U.S. Congress thanked him by awarding him the Congressional Gold Medal.

The Elachee Nature Science Center is in Gainesville. Many families visit the center to see live animals and visit special exhibits. Outdoors, they hike on wooded trails.

Providence Canyon State Park in Lumpkin is often called Georgia's Little Grand Canyon.

Many like to see the center's native plant gardens.

Parks and Festivals

Families fish, hike, and camp in Georgia's state parks. Kids can become Junior Rangers. They learn about the state's history and wildlife.

Georgia also has many festivals. The Big Pig Jig is a barbecue in Vienna. The town of Hahira has a honeybee festival every fall. The festival is full of fun. The Honeybee Parade has often been called the best parade in Georgia.

Sports

Georgia has four big-league sports teams. They are all based in Atlanta. In baseball, the Braves have appeared in several World Series. The Falcons draw football fans. The Hawks play basketball, and the Thrashers play hockey. They are named after the brown thrasher, which is the state bird.

The Peach Bowl is played in Atlanta. This is a big college football game. The University of Georgia Bulldogs have won two Peach Bowl games.

Hank Aaron is the home run king. Hammerin' Hank hit 755 homers in his twenty-three-year baseball career.

29

GLOSSARY

accused of — blamed for

civil rights — basic rights of a citizen, such as to vote, go to school, and own property

colony — a group of people living in a new land but keeping ties with the place they came from

factories — buildings where goods and products are made

gorge — a canyon, or steep-walled passage through land

Great Depression — a time in the 1930s when many people and businesses lost money

missions — churches

piedmont — an area of land lying at the foot of a mountain

retire — no longer working at a job

salt marshes — a low coastal area that sometimes gets covered with saltwater from the ocean

segregated — separated from others because of skin color

swamp — a wetland, or area that often floods, covered with trees, bushes and plants

textiles — cloth

tourists — people who travel for pleasure

Union — the United States of America

Books

James Oglethorpe. Discover the Life of a Colonial American (series). Kieran Walsh (Rourke Publishing)

Martin Luther King, Jr. People We Should Know (series) Jonatha A. Brown (Gareth Stevens)

A Net to Catch Time. Sara Harrell Banks (Knopf Books for Young Readers)

P is for Peach: A Georgia Alphabet. Carol Crane and Mark Braught (Thomson Gale)

Sequoyah : The Cherokee Man Who Gave His People Writing. James Rumford (Houghton Mifflin)

Web Sites

Arty Facts at the Telfair Museum of Art
www.telfairartyfacts.org

Coca-Cola Space Science Center
www.ccssc.org

Georgia State Parks Junior Rangers
gastateparks.org/content/georgia/pdf/jranger.pdf

Museum of Arts and Sciences
www.masmacon.com

INDEX